WELCOME, THANK YOU!

Thank you for investing in a copy of *The 100-Page Book*. I appreciate it and would like to give you access to a guide I created on *"How to Make Money With a 100-Page Book."* This valuable guide shows you 21 specific tactics and strategies to leverage your 100-page book including:

- The best photos and images to use (pages 2—5).
- The #1 "strategic" strategy for getting in front of other peoples' customers (page 8).
- My secret way to WOW! (page 10).
- How my teen daughter got front-page media coverage with her short book (page 13).
- A smart event strategy (page 16).
- A powerful type of ad to promote your book (page 22).
- And more!

DOWNLOAD TODAY!

100PageBook.com/thanks

*The Business Owner's Guide to Self-Publishing
a Short Customer Attraction Book*

THE
100-PAGE
BOOK

PROFITABLE NONFICTION BOOK WRITING TIPS

MIKE CAPUZZI

BITE SIZED
BOOKS

Bite Sized Books publishes short, helpful books or shooks™ for Main Street business owners to attract new customers. Shooks are easy-to-create, quick-to-read short books. They are designed to be read by prospective customers, clients or patients, in about an hour. Bite Sized Books offers a painless process to enable entrepreneurs and business owners to benefit from the authority that comes from being a published author, without the hassle and time commitment normally associated with writing a book. Do you have an idea for a bite sized book you would like us to publish? Visit BiteSizedBooks.com for more details.

CONTENTS

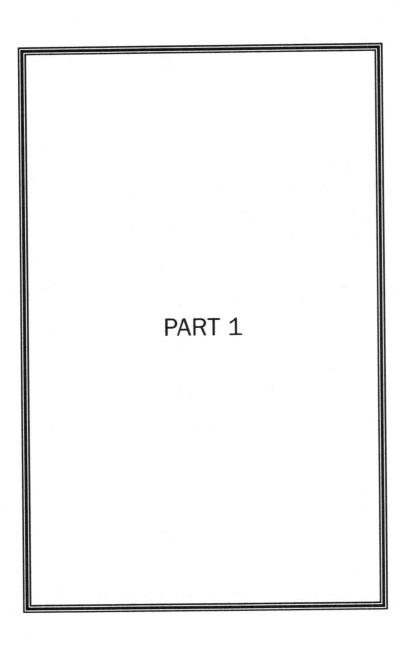

PART 1

WELCOME

AN IMPORTANT NOTE
A 100-PAGE BOOK=A "SHOOK"

Regardless if your eventual book is 100 pages, 112 pages, or 120 pages, I am going to refer to these <u>s</u>hort, <u>h</u>elpful b<u>ooks</u> as shooks™ in the rest of this shook. You can read more about how I came up with this "Capuzzi concept" starting on page 8.

Much like McDonald's has its Big Mac® and Burger King has its Whopper®, my brand of a business-oriented short, helpful book is the shook, and that is the type of book I want to help you author, publish and leverage in your business to help you attract more ideal customers.

WHO SHOULD READ
THIS BOOK?

We both know time is precious, and I surely do not want to waste your time if *The 100-Page Book* is not for you. Therefore, let me be upfront and crystal clear on exactly who I wrote this 100-page, short, helpful book (or shook™ as I call them) for.

I wrote *The 100-Page Book* for business owners and entrepreneurs who want to leverage the speed, control, and autonomy of being a self-published short, helpful book author. These men and women are local business owners, corporate executives, service providers, and online entrepreneurs.

They all have one thing in common—a belief in the power and positioning of being the author of a real, printed book, and the ability to increase the sophistication of their marketing with a book-centric marketing strategy.

What I am about to share in this shook will make many book purists cringe and shake their heads because I am going to focus 100% of my efforts here on showing you how to create a short, helpful book that is a **potent sales tool**.

If you have the ability to think outside the box and are a bit of a maverick, I wrote this book for you.

The 100-Page Book Is for the Person Who <u>Is Not</u> Concerned About:

- The do's and do not's of self-proclaimed book and literary purists.

- Writing the "perfect" book (the one that just never gets done because it's not "just right").

- Staying within the design and content confines of traditional book publishers.

- The "prestige" of being published by a big-name publisher.

- Making money by selling their books.

- Trying to achieve "best-seller" status (which these days is ubiquitous, and therefore meaningless).

- Readers reaching out directly to you and having your personal contact information.

The 100-Page Book Is for the Person Who Is Focused on:

- Speed.

- Efficiency.

- Profitability.

- A direct-response marketing architecture for the book's design and content flow.

- Being in 100% control of the book's design, content and distribution.

- Saying what you want to say and how you want to say it.

- Solving a big problem readers have or offering a big promise readers want.

- Offering helpful information first and then connecting the dots to his or her products and services.

- Enabling readers to finish the book in about an hour.

- Making money, not by selling books, but instead, by getting targeted book readers to "raise their hand" and take "the next step."

- Leveraging a shook-centric authority platform and marketing system.

Make no mistake. I am going to share with you a book creation and publishing blueprint for crafting a book that would not only make your mother proud but will also do what you want it to do, which is to position you and your business as the *go-to choice* for what it is you do.

So, if all this sounds good to you, please keep reading...

MY PROMISE TO YOU

If you are still with me, I promise not to waste the next hour or so of your life. Quite the contrary, and I truly hope this shook gives you a new option and inspiration when it comes to authoring a book for your business.

Anybody who knows me knows I tend to be direct, matter of fact and detest wasting time. If you know me, you also know I am a respected teacher and have a stellar reputation for making complex subjects easy (just do a Google search on "Mike Capuzzi" and see what others think).

I promise to do my part and give you a proven and effective strategy for authoring and publishing a short, helpful book that will position you as an authority and promote your products or services as the solution your readers need or want. I'm not going to hold anything back and will make sure you have everything you need. In return, I need you to do your part too. Make the commitment to read this shook in its entirety and with an open mind.

It is my sincerest opinion what I am about to share is:

- **The *most helpful* way to connect with potential customers.**
- The *smartest* strategy to author a book to promote you and your business.
- **The *fastest* way for you to become a published book author.**
- The *easiest* path for self-publishing a short, helpful book.

Of course, if you want or need more details than what I can include in this 100-page shook, you can check out my other shooks, *The Magic of Short Books* and *Main Street Author*.

The Magic of Short Books offers you more "how-to" detail than what I can do in this shook and gives you many examples of real-world shooks.

Main Street Author shares how local business owners (and business owners who serve them) can leverage shooks in their businesses.

You can get them on my website or from a number of online retailers.

INTRODUCTION

There are two things I want you to know about me right from the start. The first is that as of the day I am writing this, my experience with authoring and using books is 13 years and counting. The second thing is that I graduated from Penn State University with a degree in industrial engineering. This latter fact is important because industrial engineering is about making things more effective and efficient.

I published my first book, *Dream Inc.*, in 2007 and helped my first author client publish his first book in 2008. For the past 12 years, I have quietly been helping my private coaching clients build more consistent and sophisticated marketing campaigns by leveraging the power of being a published book author and expert authority.

I'm 99% positive you would have never heard of any of these individuals since they are local business owners who are only concerned with being what I call "five mile famous, " which describes the unique goal of using short, helpful books to become the #1 choice in one's local community. No concern is given to trying to be famous to everybody, everywhere, but instead, just to a select and targeted group within a specific area.

My track record of helping "everyday" business owners author, publish and leverage books is long and successful. But this is where my background in engineering kicks in. I love books. I love writing them, and I love helping others write them. But the more I got into the publishing business, the more I realized three important realities:

1. Many (nonfiction, business-oriented) books are unnecessarily bloated and are much longer than necessary.

2. While many people appreciate and want to experience the promise of books, most people never finish reading books they start.

3. People who want to write a book often start but never finish their book.

So, not being content with the norm and being motivated by Seth Godin's great little book, *Purple Cow,* I set out to address these realities.

A Purple Cow describes something phenomenal, something counterintuitive and exciting and flat-out unbelievable. In his book (which I recommend), Godin urges you to create a Purple Cow in everything you build to create something truly noticeable. This suggestion ignited my mission to create my own Purple Cow.

The result of this focused effort is the shook, which is my personal recipe and brand for a short, helpful book (with around 100 pages) focused on a nonfiction topic.

Shooks are the perfect type of book for 95% of business owners because they solve the problems that arise from the three realities I just shared.

Shooks:

1. Are focused and designed to be a conversation starter and not the entire A to Z tome on a topic.

2. Allow readers to read from cover to cover in about an hour, thereby giving them the full gist of the shook and achieving the sense of accomplishment that comes with successfully completing a task.

3. Enable everyday, normal business owners to write an effective, authority-building short book in less than two months, by following my proven, step-by-step blueprint.

If you've ever wanted to write a book to promote you and your business, but never started or completed it, or if you simply want to add a different type of book to your current library of books, *The 100-Page Book* is your passport to success!

Please note, I am going to spend zero time trying to convince you to write a book, and my assumption is if you are reading these words, you are already way past the point of having to be convinced that being a published author is an important business and position differentiator in the 21st century. My assumption is that you want to write your first book, or you are looking for smart ideas for your next book.

So, get comfortable, grab a highlighter, pen and paper, and get ready to join me for an enlightening journey. If you have any questions or comments, feel free to reach out to me at Mike@BiteSizedBooks.com, and if you want to discuss your own 100-page book with me, don't forget to schedule a Shook Strategy Session at **BiteSizedBooks.com**.

Enjoy the ride!

Mike

P.S. When you're done reading would you please leave an honest book review on Amazon? Reviews are the BEST way to help others, and I check all my reviews looking for helpful feedback. Visit:

100PageBook.com/review

REMEMBER TO GET THIS!

If you have not done so already, make sure to download the helpful guide I created for you, which details 21 smart ways to leverage a 100-page book and book-centric marketing in your business.

This is only available for a limited time!

DOWNLOAD TODAY!

100PageBook.com/thanks

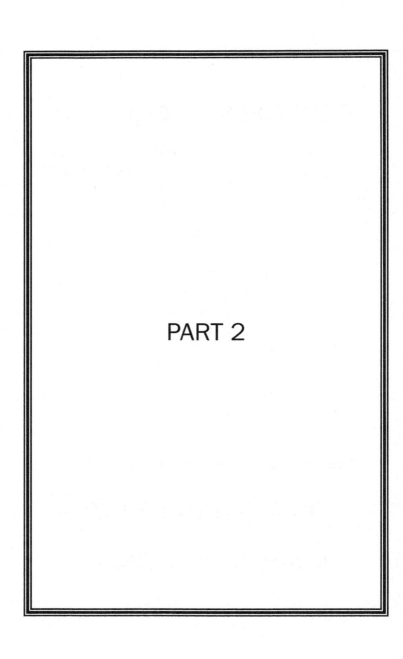

PART 2

THE 100-PAGE BOOK
BLUEPRINT

Short is the New Long

"While full-length books will never go away, there's a trend toward shorter, niche books—books that 'own' a narrow market segment. This is also a smart strategy for stretching your knowledge across multiple products."

—Penny C. Sansevieri, author of
How to Sell Books by the Truckload on Amazon

CHAPTER 1

SHOOKS ARE SMART

I want to start off by stating that I have no problem whatsoever with traditional business books that have 200, 300, or more pages. I have read hundreds of them over the years. These types of books are designed and written the way they are for a number of reasons, none of which should matter to the business owner who wants to write a book to promote his or her products and services.

In today's world, I believe authoring a shook (or better yet, a series of shooks) is a much more efficient, effective, and smarter way to leverage both printed and digital books. We all have heard the statistics about information overload and the decrease in people's attention span. Of course, social media has had a big impact, and today most people prefer to get information in bite sized chunks.

What Is a Shook?

Let me describe a few of the important details of shooks, so that you know exactly what I mean.

- They are high-quality, printed, paperback books, however, we do create e-shooks, audio shooks and "flip" shooks for online marketing.

- We use a slightly smaller "trim size" (the size of the finished book), which is 5.06" x 7.81". This smaller size makes shooks stand out and more portable.

- They typically have between 100–140 pages, however, in certain situations we can go as low as 80 pages or as many as 160. Most of my clients' shooks range between 100–128 pages. This page count allows us to have text on the cover spine so that when it sits on a shelf, somebody can find it easily.

- They contain about 12,000–15,000 words. Contrast this to a typical business book that contains 50,000 words or more.

- They are designed to be read by the average reader in 60–90 minutes, which means you can have an hour or so of "quiet time" with your readers, where they are focused on your message and getting to know you and how you can help them better.

- They take, on average, about 6–8 weeks to create from big idea to printed copies, however, the record is 22 days, held by my client, Julie Steinbacher.

- They follow a specific *helpful content* formula I have developed for optimal readability and response.

- They adhere to a specific *design* formula for maximum attention-grabbing power and physical readability.

- They are highly focused.

- Over and over again, I hear how much people love the "pithy power" of shooks.

Rather Than One Long Book, Create a Series of Shooks

Above, I mentioned my shook client, Julie Steinbacher, and you will be hearing more about her later in this shook. As of the day I am writing this, Julie has published five shooks with me, including the creation of her "*You're Not Alone*" series of three shooks for families dealing with Alzheimer's disease and dementia.

Yes, she could have written one long book covering all three topics, but chances are nobody would read the entire book, given the weighty subject matter. By breaking her subject into three shooks, it makes it much easier for her potential clients to choose which ones to read.

Julie has shared with me that she receives thank you notes from readers because she focused on making her shooks easy and friendly to read.

It's real-world feedback like this that proves to me shooks are the perfect type of book for today's consumer. I genuinely believe that many business owners would be much better suited to writing a 100-page book on a specific topic than trying to write a typical bloated book. I know their readers will surely appreciate it.

CHAPTER 2

YOUR SHOOK
IS A SALES TOOL

As we begin this journey together, I want you to understand that the type of book (ideally a shook) I am suggesting you write is first and foremost a sales tool for your business.

This requires a dramatic mind shift on how you approach writing your book and is critical to understand from the start. Whereas most nonfiction book authors are simply content to share helpful information, they make the critical mistake of not explicitly telling readers what to do next (and how to continue their relationship beyond the book).

I have seen smart marketers make this mistake and forget the true reason for authoring their book. Yes, it's about sharing helpful information, but it's also about positioning them and their products or services as the answer to what readers are seeking.

This is the essence of effective selling, and while many book purists consider such in-the-book promotion as sacrilege, I want you to think differently.

If you are going to invest your time, energy and money into authoring a shook, it absolutely must offer you a positive return on your investment that goes beyond simply being able to say you are a book author and giving copies to friends and family. Of course, it is gratifying to be able to do these, but I want to challenge you to think much bigger.

You cannot be squeamish about self-promotion and being very explicit in how you can help readers who like what you are sharing and want more from you. While I do think some marketing-oriented authors are a bit extreme with their pitches and how they aggrandize themselves, I also believe you can achieve a healthy balance of helpful information and connecting the dots for readers.

I am going to assume that whatever type of business you own or market, you help people with a specific problem or achieve a specific goal. Since your shook is going to share information, ideas, tips and guidance on a topic that is important for ideal prospects for your business, doesn't it make sense that some readers are going to want more from you? And if you fail to give them what they want, you've let them down, and they are going to seek help elsewhere.

Now is the perfect time (no pun intended) to address a common challenge many business owners face—the need for perfection, as in:

- The perfect time to get started.
- The perfect writing style.
- The perfect manuscript.

If these resonate with you, let me simply say this. You do not serve your audience by holding back until so-called perfection is obtained. There is no such thing as "perfect" when it comes to authoring and self-publishing a book—trust me on this. Everything you do will continue to evolve as you grow, but none of this will happen, including helping your ideal readers, unless you get started.

Exit Ramps for Readers

When you craft your shook correctly, readers are going to want to connect with you. I like to use the metaphor of highway exit ramps in describing this.

As people read your shook, a portion of your readers are going to want to take the first exit and immediately connect with you. They liked what they read, and they are ready to take the **Active Call-to-Action (CTA)**, as outlined in your shook.

Your Active CTA is the #1 thing you want readers, who represent ideal prospects for your business, to do. This could be scheduling a phone call or an in-person visit with you, or whatever your sales process "first step" is.

Another percentage of readers will also appreciate what you shared, but they need a bit more time and information before they reach out to you. For these readers, you want to provide what I call the **Passive CTA** and offer them opportunities for more information in exchange for their contact details.

The formula of providing *pithy*, helpful information + Active and Passive CTAs is part of what makes a shook unique. There are a few other things, like content architecture and the cover and interior design, which I will describe in more detail shortly.

For now, as you begin to plan and write your shook, I want you to keep in mind what your ultimate goal is with your shook. It's not just about being an author. It's about getting ideal readers to read your shook and then complete the Active or Passive CTA. To do this effectively, requires you to (constantly) remind yourself your shook is a sales tool, first and foremost.

CHAPTER 3

YOUR SHOOK'S
IDEAL TARGET READER

After you have wrapped your head around the fact that the book or shook you are about to write is a positioning tool for you and a sales tool for your business, the very next thing you need to consider is who your ideal target reader is.

The last thing I want you to do is write a shook for "everybody" because in terms of smart and effective marketing, "everybody" really means "nobody."

For readers, the beauty of shooks is that they are highly focused on a single topic and allow them to read the entire shook in about an hour. This laser focus means that your shook will be a perfect match for a select group of people and not "everybody." When your ideal target reader sees your book, his eyes light up and he says to himself, "This book was written for me!"

This is the emotional connection you want to make, and the only way to make it is to know who you are writing to, before you write a single word. In cases where you serve multiple audiences, my suggestion is to write a shook for each audience. You can keep a good chunk of the content the same and simply change the parts that are specific to the reader.

For example, I could take my shook, *The Magic of Short Books,* and create a series of shooks. Within a few weeks, I could have:

The Magic of Short Books for Dentists
The Magic of Short Books for Coaches
The Magic of Short Books for Insurance Agents
Etc.

Do you see the power of specificity? A dentist is not going to read the coach version, and a coach is not going to want to read the insurance agent shook.

By focusing the shook's design and content on a specific ideal target reader, you can make your shook that much more relevant and attractive to readers.

It should come as no surprise that marketing studies and my own marketing tests show that the more specific a message or content is to a target, the more likely they are to engage and respond. Writing one or a series of short, helpful books is an ideal strategy to leverage this reality.

So here is what I want you to do right now. I want you to start identifying your ideal target reader for your (first) shook. Jot down what you know about them, including things like:

- Their gender.
- What their pains are.
- What their frustrations are.
- What they want.
- What they believe.
- What they need.
- Etc.

It's important for you to have a clear picture of an ideal target reader so you can work on attracting as many as possible while simultaneously repelling those who do not fit your ideal reader profile. Remember, you don't want "everybody" to read your shook, only those who you are best meant to serve with your products and services.

The other important component to keep in mind as you work on this, is to also identify what your goals are for your shook readers.

1. What do you want your readers <u>to achieve</u> after reading your shook?

2. What do you want your readers <u>to do</u> after reading your shook?

By investing the time and energy to do this "homework" before ever writing the first words of your shook, I guarantee your shook will be that much better at connecting with the readers you want to connect with.

Once you know "who" you are writing for, the next step is to put a big idea in front of them to get them excited about what's inside your shook.

A Real-World Example

My shook client, Dominic "Slice" Teich, is an Air Force F-16 fighter pilot, who has served several tours of duty and also owns a real estate investing business.

Dom wanted to work with me to develop his first shook, which would share his tactics and strategies on how to passively invest in residential apartments.

As we began to work together, it became quite clear that while he could help just about anybody with real estate investing, Dom intuitively knew he could best serve others with a similar background as his own.

Over several coaching calls with me, his "who" became apparent to both of us, and working together we identified two ideal target readers for his shook:

1. Fighter pilots

2. Commercial pilots

Dom has a track record with helping these types of men and women successfully invest in apartment buildings and wanted to attract many more to his business.

By identifying these ideal target readers, we knew his shook should have a certain feel to both the design and style of writing.

His next task was to develop his shook hook, and I must say, I think we came up with a winner, which you can read about on page 33.

Bonus Gift!

A few years back, I created a short training titled, **The Profit-Producing, Income-Intensifying & Competition-Crushing Power of One High Impact Marketing Big Idea**.

While not specifically focused on shook authoring, I think you will find it helpful. You can download it for free and with no opt-in required by visiting:

100PageBook.com/bigidea

CHAPTER 4

YOUR SHOOK'S
BIG IDEA

If you are a serious student of marketing, I am sure you've heard of the concept of the "big idea" as it relates to how you position and promote your products and services. In his 1983 book, *Ogilvy on Advertising*, the legendary David Ogilvy shared this gem:

> "You can do homework from now until doomsday, but you will never win fame and fortune unless you also invent big ideas. It takes a big idea to attract the attention of consumers and get them to buy your product. Unless your advertising contains a big idea, it will pass like a ship in the night."

I encourage you to consider what Ogilvy is suggesting as you plan your shook and come up with your shook's big idea or shook hook as I call it.

What shook topic or focus will immediately get the attention of your ideal reader and practically make it impossible for them to NOT read your shook?

This is going to require some intentional thought and creative thinking. When I work with clients to help them write their shooks, we spend a lot of time masterminding their shook hook, so they get it right from the start.

In his recommended short book, *How to Find Your Big Marketing Idea* (which ironically is 99 pages long), Todd Brown shares 10 criteria for an effective big marketing idea. According to Brown, a big marketing idea:

1. Presents one promise.
2. Is specific.
3. Conveys one story.
4. Leads to one conclusion.
5. Taps one emotion.
6. Must be new & unique.
7. Must feel timely.
8. Is bold, captivating and arresting.
9. Is immediately understandable.
10. Is made up of one powerful idea.

I highly suggest you use these criteria to assess the big idea for your shook. Trust me, if you can develop a unique, big idea for your shook, you will have a valuable asset that will last for years.

My longtime client and shook author, Dr. Kevin Flood, created a big idea for his 100-page shook, *Are Your Teeth Toxic?: What Your Dentist Never Told You About Mercury in Your Silver Fillings.*

Kevin, who recently passed away, was a dentist who practiced mercury-free dentistry. If you are not aware, the silver amalgams used in dentistry for decades contain poisonous mercury, which has all sorts of negative effects on the body.

His shook hook focused on this danger, and the title we came up with articulates his big idea clearly. Interestingly, within the first 30 days of using his shook to market his dental practice, Kevin attracted three *new* patients, each worth thousands of dollars. This is the power of what an effective shook can do for your business.

As you brainstorm your shook's big idea, keep in mind a good shook hook should:

- Offer something that sounds "new."

- Be unique and break through the noise and clutter.

- Be clearly understood.

- Be instantly appealing (to your target reader).

I thought long and hard about the big idea behind the shook you are currently reading—*The 100-Page Book* —and time will soon tell if I have come up with a winner.

Here are some questions to ask about your targeted ideal reader to help you come up with your shook hook:

- What is keeping them awake at night?
- What are they mad about?
- What are their daily frustrations?
- What do they desire the most?
- What are they looking to achieve?

As you go through these questions, remember your ideal target reader wants to:

- Learn more about you/your business and how you can specifically help them.
- Get something they crave.
- Reduce pain, expenses, wasted time, etc.
- Gain pleasure, health, time, money, comfort, happiness, etc.

The time you invest in coming up with the big idea for your shook is a smart investment. Giving critical and creative thought to this process will ensure your shook feels unique, new, and must-read for your ideal target reader.

Don't forget to download my big idea training for free by visiting:

100PageBook.com/bigidea

A Real-World Example

On page 26, I introduced you to Dom Teich, and mentioned how he identified his two ideal target readers, which are fighter pilots and commercial pilots. After completing this step, we were able to quickly identify the "big idea" for his shook. Dom wanted to show pilots how to *build proactive wealth with passive apartment investing.*

By focusing on an extremely specific reader with a very specific promise, Dom has a powerful big idea to share. It was such a good idea that it became the basis for several concepts he trademarked for his business (Single Seat Investor™ and Proactive Wealth™) and became the title of his shook.

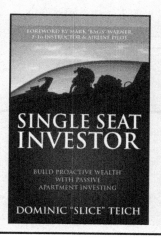 

CHAPTER 5

YOUR SHOOK'S
CALLS-TO-ACTION

S hooks are direct-response books by design. Direct response describes a form of marketing that is designed to "get a response" from the recipient. Unlike most marketing, which is typically one–way in direction to the consumer, direct-response marketing is meant as a two-way "conversation" between the sender and the recipient. The marketer sends a message with an offer and certain recipients respond.

Most nonfiction books fall into the first category— a one-way conversation. The author shares his or her information, and when the reader is done with the book, there really is nothing left for the reader to do. Instead of using the book as a conversation starter, most authors simply "talk to" their readers, and while social media has allowed many authors to build a following, this is still not the goal I suggest you try to achieve. This one-way conversation makes no sense to me, and whenever I read a book I find interesting or motivating, I always want more.

Shooks do not make this mistake. Instead, they offer readers a variety of ways to connect with the author and get additional helpful information, resources and such. I introduced you to this concept in Chapter 2 by sharing the Active and Passive Calls-to-Action, and you have already seen several examples of me doing this in this shook.

I want you to implant this Capuzzi-mantra into your author-brain: *"My shook is meant to be a conversation starter with my ideal target reader."*

Like any good conversation, it is two-way and allows both individuals to have a part in it. As the author of a shook, you must:

- Think in terms of helping before selling.

- Offer helpful information in "bite sized" chunks to make it easy and fast to read.

- Invite readers to contact you or your business.

- Offer highly motivated readers your Active CTA.

- Offer readers who want more, but are not quite ready for your Active CTA, your Passive CTA.

So, with this in mind, I want you to invest some time and energy into coming up with both the Active CTA and Passive CTA for your shook.

Since their business relies on face-to-face interactions, most local, bricks and mortar-type businesses and service business shook authors typically offer one of these types of Active CTAs:

- Call you or your business
- Visit your business
- Schedule a call with you
- Schedule a visit with you

I always suggest my shook authors share their Active CTA throughout their shook and very explicitly in what I call "The Next Step" chapter.

Typical Passive CTAs for these same types of business owners can include:

- Tip sheets
- Training resources
- Videos
- "Lost" chapters

Some authors are not concerned about getting "opt-ins" and simply repeat their Active CTA.

Your Passive CTA is all about offering additional information in return for the reader's contact details. Think about what simple and easy-to-digest information you can offer as your Passive CTA.

A Real-World Example

My Main Street Author client, Julie Steinbacher, is an elder law attorney with offices in Williamsport and State College, PA. I have had the opportunity to work with Julie for over a decade.

Julie has authored several shooks, including, *You're Not Alone: Living with Alzheimer's Disease, You're Not Alone: Living as an Alzheimer's Caregiver*, and *You're Not Alone: Living with Dementia.*

Julie has tested and used several different Passive CTAs in her shooks.

Examples of Julie's Passive CTAs

However, her Active CTA remains consistent and is always about setting up an initial consultation.

CHAPTER EIGHT

THE NEXT STEP

If you've arrived on this page after reading this entire book—thank you and congratulations. I hope I have been able to share helpful information so you realize you can live with Alzheimer's disease.

It would be an honor for me and my entire team to help you and guide you on this journey and to be there for you so you're not alone.

I know you are probably on an emotional roller-coaster right now and not sure where to start or exactly what you should do next, so here is my best advice.

Contact my office and set up a complimentary meeting with me to discuss your specific situation. It will last about 60 minutes and I will answer all your questions. At the end of the meeting, you can decide to work with me and my firm or continue on your own path.

JULIANNE I. STEINBACHER, ESQ

There is no obligation and my goal is to simply guide you on the best path for your specific needs. To schedule this complimentary meeting, please...

- Call my office at: (570) 322-2077
- Email my office at: info@paeldercounsel.com

Thank you for your time and please reach out to me so I can be of service to you.

Examples of Julie's Active CTA

Short Helpful Book (Shook) Recipe

1   Ideal target reader
1   Big Idea
2   Calls-to-action
5-7 Main content chapters
1   Next step
1   Great looking cover

Combine all ingredients into a powerful customer attractor book!

My "famous" shook recipe

CHAPTER 6

THE SHOOK RECIPE

I love to cook, and growing up in a family of good cooks, I love to eat, so it's no surprise I am a fan of using recipes to craft delicious meals. I also have an engineer's brain, therefore, checklists and clear directions are important to me, which is why I developed my own personal recipe for shooks.

I literally used this recipe to craft the shook you are now reading and explicitly use it with all my shook clients. The beauty of it is that it's simple, and even more importantly, effective.

If you decide to use it to author your own shook, I suggest you do not deviate from it. It simply works as designed. There is no need to reinvent the wheel here; just make sure your shook contains the required building blocks I am about to share.

A shook has four main parts with each part containing a set of shook building blocks (chapters) specific to that part. These parts are:

- The Cover Content.

- The Front Matter Content.

- The Main Matter Content.

- The Back Matter Content.

I go into greater detail on these shook building blocks in my shook, *The Magic of Short Books,* which you can get on my website at **MikeCapuzzi.com** or via number of online retailers.

Cover Content

☐ Professional design—a must!

☐ Front cover and spine details—your shook's front cover is where you get the opportunity to make a powerful first impression, and unless you are a graphic designer yourself, you want to let a professional create your shook cover. Using the right graphics, fonts and other details is critically important, and you don't want to be sloppy or cheap about this. As far as the spine, you want to have your title and your name on it. Your goal is to make it easy to find your shook on a bookshelf.

☐ Effective, attention-grabbing title and sub-title—crafting your shook's title and subtitle is an iterative and important process. It's similar to developing a strong headline when copywriting and requires time, work and rework to get it right. The good news is if you've identified your targeted reader and your hook, creating an attention-grabbing title that practically forces people to want to read your shook is simple.

☐ Back cover details—the back cover is the final piece of the three parts of your shook cover (front, spine and back).

Regarding the back cover, here are some smart things to include:

- Strong *reason to read* headline
- Shook description including a few specific *here's what's inside* bullets
- V.I.P. testimonial
- Reader reviews/testimonials
- Short author bio and photo
- Main website or shook-focused site URL
- QR code to website
- ISBN and barcode (if selling via retail)
- Price and book category

Front Matter Content

☐ Reader Bonus/Gift Offer—we've finally gotten to the first page of your shook. This is the right-hand side page that is first seen when somebody opens your shook. In many books, this page is left blank or is the title page. In a shook, this page is specifically designed to be a reader bonus/gift page where readers can get a valuable bonus/gift (your Passive CTA).

☐ Also By page—this is an optional page, but if you've created other books, reports, trainings, etc., you should include them on this page.

☐ Title page—your title page includes your title, subtitle and name. I like to design this page so that it leaves room for you to write a personal note and autograph your shooks.

☐ Testimonial page(s)—this is an optional page, but if you have testimonials/reviews of your shook, you should include them here. The way you get them is to give out pre-release copies to specific individuals and ask them to write a short testimonial about the shook. Be strategic about who you ask to review.

☐ Copyright page—this page includes all copyright information, disclaimers, publisher details and important legal information.

☐ Dedication page—this is an optional page that allows you to dedicate your shook to an important person or persons, a group of people, specific niche, etc.

☐ Acknowledgements page—this is an optional page that allows you to acknowledge and thank people who were helpful to you in creating your shook.

☐ Table of Contents—the table of contents is an important part of your shook and should entice readers to want to read it. Make sure you check and double-check the titles and page numbers to make sure they are correct before going to print.

Main Matter Content

☐ Foreword—this is an optional page, but if it makes sense and you can find a V.I.P. to write the foreword to your shook, it can make it that much more powerful. When thinking about a person to write it, consider who you would like to have associated with your shook and who may be inclined to share it with their circles of influence simply because they were asked to write the foreword. If you cannot find a notable V.I.P., consider asking a valuable customer to write it for you.

☐ Who Should Read This Book?—this is an optional chapter but one I personally like to include, like I did in this shook. I like to be upfront and transparent with my shook's goals and exactly who I created it for. While I appreciate people who are interested in my shook, if they don't fit the profile of the types of business owners I'm looking to attract and work with, they do me little good. This chapter allows me to boldly proclaim who should and should not read my shook. In turn, this will strengthen the bond with my target readers, since they know I wrote it specifically for them.

☐ My Promise to You—this is an optional chapter but one I believe you should include. Starting your shook off with a bold promise is a smart way to keep you focused on what you must deliver and prepare your readers for what to expect. Few business owners set any sort of lofty expectation these days, so making a promise from the beginning shows you are different than the masses.

☐ Introduction—I recommend all shook authors start their shook with a "reason why" introduction that articulates the reason(s) why you are publishing it. Let your readers know what they will get by reading it, why it's different, and why it's important they read it now. An excellent book recommendation for crafting your "why" is *Start with Why* by Simon Sinek. I found this book to be an excellent reminder when creating any type of marketing message.

☐ Main Chapters—this is where you include your main content chapters. Remember, these are bite sized chunks of information focused on helping the reader with your shook hook. The typical length of these chapters is 1,000–2,500 words depending on how many you have. I try to limit the number of content chapters to no more than seven (though I was not able to do that with this shook). Remember, shooks are NOT meant to teach readers everything you know about the topic. They are meant to provide valuable information and then guide the reader to the next step, which is typically reaching out and contacting you.

Back Matter Content

☐ Product & Service Information—this chapter represents a "bridge" between your content chapters and your "selling" chapters. Up to this point, you have shared helpful information and now its time to connect the dots for your readers and share with them how you specifically help your customers. This should be a big, bold chapter which positions you and your business as the logical, go-to choice.

☐ The Next Step—it's critical your shook tells readers the next thing they must do in order to achieve the goal they were seeking when they first picked it up. Remember this is your Active CTA, and it's the #1 thing you want the reader to do after reading your shook. I like to keep this limited to one thing, so it's clear and simple to do. Depending on your business, it could be to call you, visit you, fill out a survey, etc. Give detailed instructions on what to do next if they want to solve their problem or achieve their goal.

☐ Author Biography—include your bio and important details about your background, experience, etc. This allows your readers to get to know you better. If you don't have professionally shot photographs, now is a good time to get them done.

☐ About the Business—this is an optional chapter depending on your business. If your business is a destination for consumers or has a long history in your community, I would definitely include this chapter.

- ☐ Frequently Asked Questions—this is an optional chapter, but if you have many typical questions prospects ask you, including them in your shook is helpful.

- ☐ Author Resources—this is an optional page, but if you have other resources you would like readers to know about, include them here.

- ☐ Glossary/Bibliography—this is an optional chapter, but if you have technical jargon and specific language in your business, consider including a glossary to help readers. If your shook includes researched information or data, considering including a bibliography to inform readers on how widely you researched the topic.

- ☐ Companion Book to This Book—if you have another book readers should definitely check out, include a cover image and short preview of it here.

- ☐ Reader Bonus/Gift Offer—depending on your shook's page count (all printed books must have a page count divisible by four, e.g., 104 pages, 108 pages, 112 pages, etc.), you may have a blank last even-numbered page. Rather than let this go to waste, I suggest repeating the same reader bonus/gift offer that started your shook.

No Need to Reengineer This!

What I have just shared with you is a powerful and effective recipe for your shooks. It follows a classic, direct-response marketing formula and it works great. You can see how I use it in this shook and any of my other shooks. It's also the exact recipe I follow when working on a client's shook, so there is no need to deviate from it.

Just remember, your shook is a conversation starter. It is not meant to be the entire A to Z dissertation on your topic. Therefore, keeping the content focused and flowing smoothly is important.

If you want to discuss how to apply all this to your shook, schedule a Shook Strategy Session with me by visiting **BiteSizedBooks.com**.

CHAPTER 7

YOUR SHOOK'S OUTLINE

Now that you know what goes into a shook, your next step is to create an outline for it. This outline will eventually become your Table of Contents for your shook. This is the last step before starting the content creation phase.

I like to keep things simple, and I use a Microsoft Excel® spreadsheet to develop my shook outline. You can see a screenshot of the actual spreadsheet I used to write this shook on the next page.

While this simple step may feel unnecessary, I find it to be a vital step to keep focused on the exact flow and content of your shook. As the saying goes, "You can't hit a target you have not identified." By creating your outline first, you can identify which parts you want to include and exclude and the high-level overview of your shook.

TITLE:	The 100-Page Book	
Section	Buiding Block	Word Count
FRONT MATTER	Reader Bonus page	
FRONT MATTER	Title page	
FRONT MATTER	Copyright page	
FRONT MATTER	Table of Contents	
MAIN MATTER	Who Should Read This Book?	480
MAIN MATTER	My Promise	320
MAIN MATTER	Introduction	752
MAIN MATTER	Chapter 1: Shooks Are Smart	597
MAIN MATTER	Chapter 2: Your Shook is a Sales Tool	614
MAIN MATTER	Chapter 3: Your Shook's Ideal Reader	796
MAIN MATTER	Chapter 4: Your Shook's Big Idea	773
MAIN MATTER	Chapter 5: Your Shook's Calls-to-Action	570
MAIN MATTER	Chapter 6: The Shook Recipe	1510
MAIN MATTER	Chapter 7: Your Shook's Outline	142
MAIN MATTER	Chapter 8: Crafting Your Shook's Content	638
MAIN MATTER	Chapter 9: Designing & Printing Your Shook	1376
MAIN MATTER	Chapter 10: Your Shook Is Your Business Card	268
MAIN MATTER	Chapter 11: Bite Sized Books	839
BACK MATTER	Chapter 12: The Next Step	273
BACK MATTER	Resources for Authors	103
BACK MATTER	Frequently-Asked Questions	1935
BACK MATTER	About Mike Capuzzi	240
BACK MATTER	The Main Street Author Podcast	116
BACK MATTER	A Small Favor	127
		11,989

Knowing exactly what to write about in the Main Matter of your shook takes a bit more consideration and is something I work on closely with my clients.

If you are looking for a simple, yet effective formula for your Main Matter content, I suggest you come up with 5—7 frequently-asked questions, should-ask questions, secrets, tips, or ideas that an ideal customer would find useful and write your chapters around this content.

By "chunking" your content into 5—7 (or 10) main ideas, you are making it easy for your readers to read your shook and making it easier on you to write it. You can see a real-world example of this with the very shook you are reading right now!

CHAPTER 8

CRAFTING YOUR SHOOK'S CONTENT

I t's time to start crafting the content of your shook. Notice I did not say "writing the content," since these days, there are several options available to you for getting the words out of your head and into a printed shook. As far as ways to create the main content, here are several strategies for crafting it. These are in order of my personal preference.

WRITE IT—the traditional method of writing your shook's content is, in my opinion, the best way to create your shook if you enjoy writing and are decent at it. I get that it can feel like a daunting task, but I believe sitting down and actually writing your content will pay off in many different ways in your business. I have seen amazing new ideas birth and grow from this process, and many of my clients thank me for encouraging them to write their own shook.

During this process, you will see holes in your messaging and develop new and better ways to describe your solutions. No other person is as passionate and interested in your topic as you are, so if you can set time aside and use this shook as your blueprint, I know you can do it.

I literally shut myself in my office for a few days and crafted most of the content for this shook. Of course, I had properly outlined my thoughts and planned before sequestering myself, but I was able to complete most of this shook's content in a single, focused day. I am not saying you need to do the same thing, but there is something powerful about getting away from your day-to-day distractions to make yourself exceptionally productive.

PRESENT IT—if you do face-to-face presentations or even virtual webinar-based talks, your 60-minute presentation could make the perfect content for your shook. The skills necessary to craft a compelling presentation, including the flow and content, are the same skills needed to create a good shook. Essentially, you deliver your presentation, record it and then have it transcribed so that it can be edited into its final format.

TALK IT—another book-authoring strategy that is popular these days is to talk your book out on your smart phone or computer, have it transcribed and then polished by a professional writer. For some, it might be easier to talk your shook out instead of sitting down at a computer. There are several online services for transcription, which make this once expensive and tedious task much easier.

REPURPOSE IT—if you have lots of content you've previously written, you can repurpose it for your shook, saving you hours of time and energy. For example, if you have been writing blog content for years, you can take selected blog posts and use them as the main content of your shook. You could also convert videos and podcasts you have recorded into useable content.

HIRE IT—a final strategy and one I used to create my first book, *Dream Inc.*, was to find and hire a professional ghostwriter to interview each of the 31 contributors and write their chapter based on the interview content. You could hire a ghostwriter to interview you and write your shook's content. Just be aware that a professional ghostwriter is a substantial investment.

PROOFREADING—when your shook's manuscript is finished, it's important you have it proofread and copyedited by an experienced set of eyes. While it's almost impossible to publish any type of book that has no errors in it, you do want to do your best to minimize grammar and content mistakes, which is why you need to find an experienced proofreader/ copyeditor to review your manuscript.

If you don't have this type of resource, visit **Upwork.com** or **Guru.com** and do a search. Just make sure the person you hire is experienced and performs quality work.

CHAPTER 9

DESIGNING AND PRINTING YOUR SHOOK

The days of painstakingly typesetting a book are long over, and with the advent of digital, print-on-demand book printing, you have the amazing opportunity to author, design and print your own shooks. Also long gone are the days where you had to order thousands of printed books. These days, you can order as few as one copy of your printed shook.

Designing Your Shook

There are two unique design components of any book—the cover design and the interior design. And while software tools have made it easy for just about anybody to design their shook, this doesn't mean anybody should do the design.

I have seen countless books that break all sorts of book design rules (yes, they exist) and simply look bad. You only get one chance to make a first impression, and I believe an amateur or poor design will hurt you and your business brand.

The cover design and interior design each have their own unique suggested guidelines and design requirements, and a person who is good at cover design doesn't necessarily mean they are good at interior design. My suggestion is to always work with a good book cover design professional and a good book interior design professional.

For my independent publishing company, Bite Sized Books, we have both cover designers and interior designers. We also follow a specific design look and feel for the shooks we publish. I share these details, in-depth, in *The Magic of Short Books*. I feel strongly about what makes for good book design, and we work hard to make sure our shooks are great-looking and easy to read.

But since this is a *"how to"* shook, let me share the various design alternatives you have.

Essentially, you have three options when it comes to designing your shook's cover and interior.

1. Do-it-yourself.

2. Hire a cover designer and interior designer.

3. Work with a publisher.

Let's take a quick look at each of these strategies and you can decide for yourself the best choice.

DO IT YOURSELF—if you have a design background or enjoy doing layout work, you can design your own shook cover and design the interior using any number of software programs available. While I do not recommend it (because it is not easy), you can even design your entire book in a tool as simple as Microsoft Word. The range of software tools for doing shook interior design runs from the basic (Microsoft Word or Microsoft Publisher) all the way up to professional-level products like Adobe InDesign and Quark Xpress.

Amazon KDP has several free software tools available, and a quick Google search on "book interior design templates" will result in a variety of templates available for the do-it-yourselfer. Also, a number of book printers have their own online design tools available.

I will restate my warning again. Unless you have a good eye for book design, I would not recommend trying to design your own shook. There are too many pitfalls and mistakes you can make. Stay focused on everything I have shared so far, and work with a pro to make your shook look great!

HIRE A COVER & INTERIOR DESIGNER— if you still want to do your shook yourself, but do not have the necessary design skills, then hiring an independent cover designer and interior designer is a good choice. While many designers may tell you they do both cover and interior design, I think both are a unique specialty and each requires a specialist. If you decide to work with a single designer, just make sure you have seen their portfolio of cover and interior designs.

You can find book designers on sites like **Guru.com** and **Upwork.com**. You can also use design contest sites like **99Designs.com**, **DesignHill.com** and **DesignCrowd.com**. While you will typically pay more for using a design contest site, the upside is that you will get a number of designers creating ideas and bidding on your project. The downside to this (if it can be called a downside) is that you will have to wade through a bunch of designs and choose a winner. This is harder than it sounds.

WORK WITH A PUBLISHER—all quality book publishers will have professional cover and interior designers available for their authors, and if you go this route, you can rest assure you will be in good hands.

One last comment on the design of your shook—I always like to see what other authors of similar books have done for design inspiration. There is nothing wrong with perusing **Amazon.com** or your local book store to get design ideas for your shook.

Printing Your Shook

As I mentioned earlier, the book printing industry has transformed over the past decade, and what was once a costly and time-dependent effort has become cost-effective and fast.

To give you an idea of this transformation, in 2007, I had to order 3,000 copies of my first book, *Dream, Inc.*, in order to get the price point to where I wanted it. That is a big upfront amount, not to mention storage issue.

These days, I can upload a book to Amazon via its Kindle Direct Publishing (KDP) program and have as few as one copy in my hands within two weeks. All without any upfront money, other than the expense of creating the shook. If you decide to use KDP, you can upload your book for free and then print as many author copies as you want (my suggestion is to do small batches in case you find a mistake or something you want to edit).

Just like with design, you essentially have three options available to you for printing :

1. Use a digital book printer.
2. Use a self-publishing platform.
3. Work with a publisher.

Like before, let's take a more in-depth look at each so you can decide the best route for you.

USE A DIGITAL BOOK PRINTER—there are many book-printing companies that service authors and publishers. These companies are no different than other printing companies, except they specialize in producing quality paperback and hardcover books, and their level of service typically end when the book is printed. Examples of digital, print-on-demand book printers include companies like Steuben Press, DiggyPOD, and Gorham Printing.

USE A SELF-PUBLISHING PLATFORM—over the past several years, a number of self-publishing companies have started and offer a higher level of service than a company that just does printing. A quick Google search on "digital book printing" will give you a long list to check out. Here's a few companies I've heard good things about: **Lulu.com**, **48HourBooks.com**, and **BookBaby.com**.

I would also consider Amazon KDP, Apple Books, Ingram Spark, Barnes & Noble Press and several other similar companies to fall in this category.

WORK WITH A PUBLISHER—if you decide to work with a publisher, albeit an independent one like my company or a traditional one, they will be able to print your shook at a high level of quality. One key difference to be aware of between using a book publisher and the other options is that often a book publisher will retain the rights to your book, and you will be required to order books directly from them. I do not do this with my authors, and I instruct them to use the path that best serves their needs.

Final Thoughts on Design and Printing

Authoring, designing and printing a high-quality shook that looks and feels great is well within your reach. Given the amount of space I have here, I can only scratch the surface of all the options available to you. I do go into more detail in my shook, *The Magic of Short Books*, which you can get on my website or Amazon.

I will also leave you with these final thoughts:

- You want your shook to look great, so don't be cheap about this or try to do it yourself if you don't have a high level of design capabilities.

- Get inspired by what others have done, and make sure you adhere to traditional book design principles.

- Print your shooks with a quality book printer.

- Work with professionals to ensure your shook is the best it can be!

- Schedule a Shook Strategy Session with me to discuss all this. There is no cost or obligation. Visit **BiteSizedBooks.com**.

CHAPTER 10

YOUR SHOOK
IS YOUR BUSINESS CARD

B ack in Chapter 2, I discussed how the type of book I think you should author is first and foremost a sales tool for you and your business. So it should come as no surprise when I tell you that writing, designing and printing your book is the *easy* part. What is more challenging is the focused and consistent use of your shook within what I call a *shook-centric marketing system*. While it's outside the realm of this shook, let me share some practical and smart advice on how to best leverage your shook.

It is critical that you remind yourself that a box of unused shooks, sitting in storage closet, is not doing anybody any good. Smart authors are constantly figuring out ways to leverage their shook and get it in front of the right audience. Use it like you would a business card, and do not be afraid to give it away to qualified prospects. If you are a local business owner, you have several unique opportunities to leverage a shook in your community. I illustrate many of these in my helpful guide, *How to Make Money With a 100 -Page Book*, which you can download for free at **100PageBook.com/thanks**.

In this guide, I have identified 21 powerful tactics to leverage a shook and create a shook-centric marketing system in your business. These tactics are ideal for authors who are local business owners, professional practice owners, coaches and consultants, service providers, etc.

It's free, it's valuable, and it will open your eyes to new opportunities to promote your business. Visit **100PageBook.com/thanks**.

CHAPTER 11

BITE SIZED BOOKS

Bite Sized Books is the name of my shook publishing venture where I help business owners who want to leverage the power of a shook in their business. Shooks are bite sized books in size and in the way they convey information.

I created Bite Sized Books because I believe many business owners would be much better suited to publishing a shook or series of shooks instead of the traditional 200+ page book that takes a long longer to read and a lot longer to write.

This is a WIN-WIN for both your readers and you, and as way to further inspire you to think about crafting your own short, helpful book, I want to share a few real-world shook examples from everyday business owners from around the world.

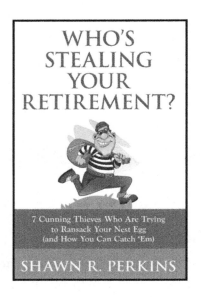

Title: *Who's Stealing Your Retirement?*

Subtitle: *7 Cunning Thieves Who Are Trying to Ransack Your Nest Egg (and How You Can Catch 'Em)*

Author: Shawn R. Perkins, financial planner

Shook hook: Discover seven major mistakes you can make with retirement planning and how to prevent them

Page count: 100

Active CTA: Schedule a Discovery Call

Passive CTA: Download two valuable "bonus" chapters

Title: *Sleep Better*

Subtitle: n/a

Author: Jeff Giagnocavo, mattress retailer

Shook hook: Discover simple ways to improve your sleep

Page count: 104

Active CTA: Visit his store and get a free custom pillow

Passive CTA: Repeat Active CTA

Title: *Help More People & Make More Money*

Subtitle: *How Offering Alzheimer's and Dementia Planning Services Helps Others and Profits Your Practice*

Author: Julieanne E. Steinbacher

Shook hook: Designed to be given away at an event with elder law lawyers where Julie was speaking, it shares ways lawyers can offer new services to clients

Page count: 100

Active CTA: Free three-month test drive of Julie's program

Passive CTA: Repeat Active CTA

Title: *Zero Bars*

Subtitle: *How Poor Indoor Cell Phone Reception Impacts Your Business and What You Can Do to Eliminate It Forever*

Author: Bob Von Stein

Shook hook: Discover how poor indoor cell reception affects your business and how you can solve this problem

Page count: 100

Active CTA: Schedule a free consultation

Passive CTA: Repeat Active CTA

Title: *Virtual Events Made Easy*

Subtitle: *How to Plan, Promote, & Profit From Live, Virtual Events with 10 to 100,000 Attendees*

Author: Greg Russell

Shook hook: COVID-19 has changed the rules of events—see how you can succeed with virtual events

Page count: 112

Active CTA: Schedule an introductory call

Passive CTA: Download a resource list of the best virtual event platforms

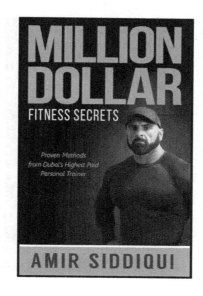

Title: *Million Dollar Fitness Secrets*

Subtitle: *Proven Methods from Dubai's Highest Paid Personal Trainer*

Author: Amir Siddiqui

Shook hook: Discover seven major mistakes you can make with retirement planning and how to prevent them

Page count: 104

Active CTA: Schedule a free Transformation Consultation

Passive CTA: Download a valuable 12-week exercise and diet plan

Title: *White Label CRM Success*

Subtitle: *The Essential Guide to Your Own Branded CRM and Creating Clients for Life*

Author: Jeff Shamus

Shook hook: Discover the power and profitability of creating your own branded CRM system

Page count: 124

Active CTA: Schedule a Discovery Call

Passive CTA: Download a White Label CRM score-card to see how ready you are for a White Label CRM solution

Title: *Got Physical Empowerment?*

Subtitle: *The Ambitious Woman's Guide to Living a Kickass Life*

Author: Rich Kohler

Shook hook: Discover Rich's mental and physical strategies that physically empower women to achieve new levels of success

Page count: 108

Active CTA: Join the online community of Hands Off Lady Rebels

Passive CTA: Download a bonus video training

Title: *IRS Problems Solved*

Subtitle: *The Ultimate Guide to Resolving Your Tax Debt by an Experienced Tax Attorney Who Knows the Ins and Outs of the IRS*

Author: Markwei Boye, Esq.

Shook hook: Discover proven ways to get out of trouble with the IRS

Page count: 108

Active CTA: Schedule a consultation

Passive CTA: Download a report on *"How To Get The IRS to Reduce or Remove Penalties and Interest"*

Title: *Are Your Teeth Toxic?*

Subtitle: *What Your Dentist Never Told You About Mercury in Your Silver Fillings*

Author: Dr. Kevin Flood, DDS

Shook hook: Silver amalgams contain dangerous mercury and why you should have them removed

Page count: 108

Active CTA: Save 50% on an initial patient visit

Passive CTA: Repeat Active CTA

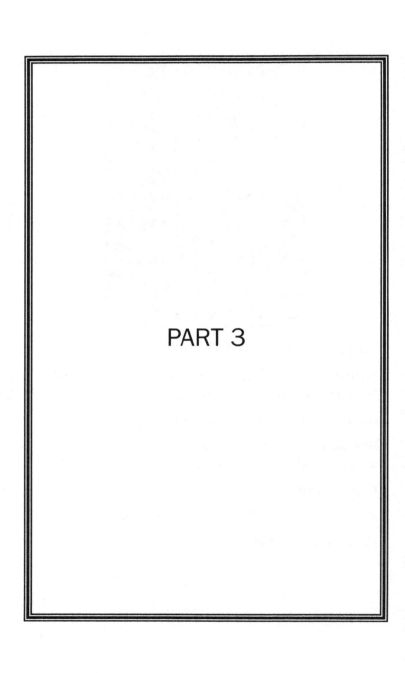

PART 3

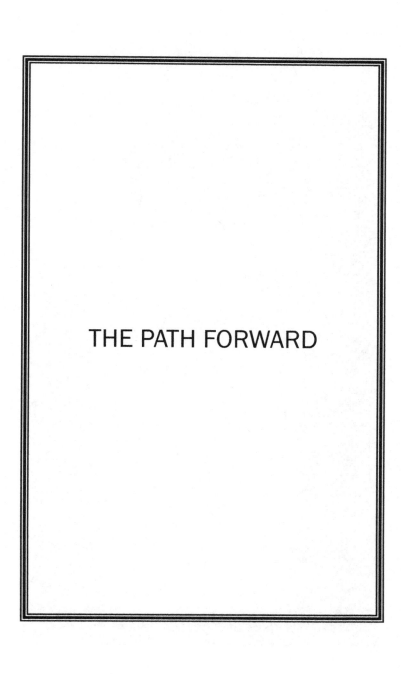

THE PATH FORWARD

CHAPTER 12

THE NEXT STEP

Congratulations, you've almost finished this shook. I hope by now you're convinced a shook is a must-have valuable asset for you and your business. I hope I have inspired you to think about multiple shooks you can create for your business—each addressing a specific issue you can help people with.

I wrote *The 100-Page Book* to be a starting point for our relationship, and as I see it, you have three opportunities in front of you right now.

1. You can close this shook and do nothing with the information I shared. If you have gotten this far, I surely hope this is not an option.

2. You can start on your shook on your own leveraging the tips, tactics and strategies I have just given you.

3. You can make the wise decision to schedule a Shook Strategy Session with me to discuss your nonfiction business book ideas. There is no obligation. Scheduling it is super easy, and really, what do you have to lose? Maybe we are meant to work together. Maybe not. But we will not know unless you have a conversation. Visit **BiteSizedBooks.com** to easily schedule this complimentary call.

I Know You Have a Shook In You!

The choice is yours, and regardless of which path you take, I truly hope I have inspired you to start working on your own 100-page book!

Remember, you are not serving your audience to your best ability if you don't have a short, helpful book written specifically for them.

If I can be of service to you, please let me know and best wishes as you move forward.

Mike Capuzzi
Mike@BiteSizedBooks.com

HELPFUL RESOURCES FOR SHOOK AUTHORS

Mike's Shooks

MikeCapuzzi.com or Amazon.com

- *The 100-Page Book*
- *The Magic of Short Books*
- *Main Street Author*
- *High Impact Marketing Manifesto*
- *Just Do This*

Training Resources

The Main Street Author Roadmap available at MainStreetAuthor.com

Mike's Helpful Marketing Tips

MikeCapuzzi.com

Main Street Author Podcast

On The Main Street Author Podcast, I interview everyday business owners who are authors and are using books as marketing tools. You can listen to episodes on any number of podcast platforms or visit MikeCapuzzi.com.

Writing and Editing Resources

- Guru.com
- Upwork.com

Writing and Editing Resources

- Guru.com
- Upwork.com
- 99Designs.com
- DesignHill.com
- DesignCrowd.com

Book Printing Resources

- KDP.Amazon.com
- IngramSpark.com
- SteubenPress.com
- DiggyPOD.com
- GorhamPrinting.com
- Lulu.com
- 48HourBooks.com
- BookBaby.com

FREQUENTLY ASKED QUESTIONS

I often get the same type of questions when speaking with business owners who are interested in creating a shook, so I thought I would include some of those questions here to help you get an even better understanding of how we can work together.

"MIKE, HOW IS THIS DIFFERENT FROM EVERYTHING ELSE I'VE SEEN?"

Shooks are radically different than typical business books and follow a specific "recipe" that I've perfected after much trial and error.

Shooks are "books without bloat," which means they don't contain the fluff and unnecessary content many typical books contain to increase page count.

For your intended reader, shooks are designed to be read in about an hour, and they offer a clear "next step."

Shooks are a different size and page count compared to typical business books which means they stand out and create a "pattern interrupt."

A pattern interrupt is something that is different and unique and grabs attention, which is important for getting your book noticed!

Shooks are direct-response books and follow a specific formula for engaging readers and inviting them to take "the next step."

Everything about a shook is perfect for today's time-strapped consumer who is looking for helpful information on a specific topic of interest but doesn't want to spend days or weeks reading a bloated book.

For you, the author, shooks are the IDEAL type of book to author, publish and leverage in your business!

My foolproof, paint-by-numbers system guarantees your shook will be done, from start to finish, in three months or less.

You will work directly with me as your coach, guide and accountability partner to make sure your shook looks great and does what it's supposed to do!

I know of no other publishing opportunity that combines the power of a shook with a simple, step-by

-step publishing program designed specifically for Main Street business owners.

"MIKE, WHAT'S IN IT FOR ME?"

It is my sincerest belief that being a published author is the key to being recognized as a significant, respected and valued expert in your community or niche. I also believe that publishing a short, helpful book is the KEY to attracting new customers instead of pursuing them.

It's a fact that people treat published authors with high levels of respect, and it all starts with being a Main Street Author.

Being a Main Street Author:

- Increases your name recognition.

- Enhances your reputation.

- Boots believability.

- Builds trust.

- And establishes authority.

Remember, people throw away brochures, advertisements and other typical forms of marketing.

People don't throw away books.

"MIKE, HOW DO I KNOW THIS IS FOR REAL?"

To date, I've published 10 of my own short, helpful books, and I've helped more than 50 traditional,

Main Street business owners' author and publish their own shooks. Here are just a few of them.

Julie Steinbacher, an elder law attorney who authored two shooks for families who are experiencing the effects of Alzheimer's disease. Within the first few months of promoting these shooks in her community, she had over 70 requests for copies and turned 10 of these requests into new clients worth over $40,000 to her firm. Due to the success of these two shooks, Julie is created her third shook, one focused on dementia.

Dr. Kevin Flood, a dentist, published a shook on the dangerous effects of mercury in your mouth. Within the first 30 days of using his shook in his local community, Kevin attracted three new patients.

Jeff Giagnocavo created a shook for helping other mattress retailers. Jeff was a keynote speaker at a mattress retailer seminar and gave away copies of this shook. During the event, he attracted two new consulting clients, worth over $10,000 each for his consulting business.

My reputation for client service and getting things done right is second to none.

"MIKE, WHERE DO I START?"

If you've always wanted to author a book for you and your business but you're not sure how or where to start (or you did start your book but never finished it), that's OK and I get it.

There is a lot of confusing information, and frankly bad advice being shared by other publishers, online "gurus" and so-called "experts."

Having the book-publishing strategy that ideally fits you and your business is a vital key. The strategies for the person who wants to make money by selling books or who is aspired to be a bestselling author are not necessarily the right strategies for the business owner who is looking to attract customers in his or her community. That is why I have developed the shook and the Main Street Author Programs.

My aim is to give Main Street business owners and business owners who serve Main Street business owners the best type of book for their consumers and the fastest and easiest path to authoring it.

Working together, **I KNOW YOU CAN DO THIS!**

"MIKE, WHY IS THIS SO IMPORTANT TO ME RIGHT NOW?"

Study any recognized authority and chances are they have published a book (or several books).

Recently, I spoke with an established insurance agent (let's call him Pat) who was interested in publishing a shook. His business was flat, and the increase in local competition was having a dramatic impact on his ability to attract new clients.

He believed publishing a shook could be the gamechanger he needed, but he allowed his habit of in-decision and giving his office manager control of his marketing decisions to push off the decision for an entire year, when "things should be better."

My response back was something to the effect of...

"Pat, if your business growth is flat (and getting flatter), don't you think it's important to do something **DRAMATICALLY DIFFERENT NOW**?"

I am afraid Pat's business is not going to be much different a year from now. In my opinion, every day you don't have a shook working for you and your business is a day of missed opportunity.

If you don't draw a line in the sand, at this very moment, and promise yourself that today is the day to get started on the path of being a Main Street author, you risk being like Pat.

Don't be like Pat.

Schedule a Shook Strategy Session with me and let's mastermind your short, helpful book!

"MIKE WHY SHOULD I TRUST YOU?"

Because I've been in your shoes and know what it's like to want to write a book but not know where or how to start.

And this is why I worked so hard to develop the shook format formula and perfect the Main Street Author Programs.

Go ahead and Google "Mike Capuzzi" and see what you find.

I have spoken for and worked with some of the world's most recognized and respected marketing experts and my reputation is stellar.

Working with me is simple, efficient and most importantly, you have the peace of mind knowing you are working with a 20+ year marketing and publishing expert.

When your shook is done, it will be a valuable business ASSET that will work for you 24 hours a day, 7 days a week helping to attract and convert new customers.

"MIKE, HOW DO YOUR SHOOK PUBLISHING PROGRAMS WORK?"

My Main Street Author Programs are turnkey shook-authoring and publishing programs unlike anything else I am aware of out there.

We literally work together over the course of 8–12 weeks to plan, author, publish and leverage your shook.

Every part of your shook is designed and authored to my exact specifications, and every step of the authoring and publishing process is designed to make this as painless and simple for you as possible.

This prevents missteps and mistakes and ensures a smooth authoring and publishing process and a great-looking shook you and your family will be proud of!

"MIKE, HOW CAN I GET STARTED?"

Review the current Main Street Author Programs at **MainStreetAuthor.com.** Whereas other similar publishing opportunities have a price tag of $10,000, $25,000 and more, my programs are priced fairly and offer you immense value.

Even if you were to do everything by yourself (which I don't recommend), you would be hard-pressed to be able to author and publish your shook for much less.

The next step is to schedule a complimentary Shook Strategy Session with me to discuss your shook ideas.

Now let me ask YOU a question...

"WHAT DO YOU HAVE TO LOSE?"

Look, you have seen how I and others have authored, published and leveraged short, helpful books to become a recognized expert and attract (versus pursue) new customers.

You have heard how others who have used my proven shook formula and Main Street Author publishing process who are now authors and reaping the benefits of being a published author.

I've put together a transparent and value-packed set of shook-publishing options designed specifically for local business owners and the business owners who serve local business owners.

Now it's time for a decision.

The way I see it, you have three options.

Option #1 is to do absolutely nothing and stay exactly where you are now.

If you aren't convinced that being a published author is important and critical in today's business environment, then maybe you don't need my proven Main Street Author strategy.

But if you understand the magic of being a published author and like to avoid mistakes and get your shook done quickly and efficiently, you have two other options.

Option #2 is to plan, write, publish and leverage your shook by yourself.

You can do all the big and little things yourself.

You can go find a book interior designer and cover designer on your own.

You can hire a copyeditor to proof your manuscript.

You can put together your own book-centric marketing strategy.

And if you are willing to work hard and spend weeks in front of your computer, you might be able to pull it off.

Option #3 is to let me do the heavy lifting for you.

I'll put my proven shook and Main Street Author publishing formulas to work for you.

I will show you what to do and how to craft your shook's content in the IDEAL way.

I will make sure your finished shook looks great.

I will show you how to use it in your business to attract and convert new customers—all in a matter of a few weeks.

Of these three options, ask yourself...

"What's going to be easier for me?"

You see, there are two types of people in the world:

1. Those who only dream about being a published author without ever taking any action to make it happen

2. Those who are ready to act when the opportunity presents itself

Many people will tell you they want to become an author and write a book.

But we both know very few actually make it happen.

It's the nature of people.

It's the classic tale of the willful and the wishful.

Most people will keep dreaming, while the few who are serious about becoming a published author and becoming a significant, respected and valued expert in their community will take action.

Since you've read this far, I think you are one of the few special ones.

I think you are one of the handful of business owners I am looking for to become the next Main Street Author. If I am right and you're still with me...

Schedule a Shook Strategy Session with me to get started on the profitable path of being a Main Street Author. This will give us a chance to "meet" and see if working together makes sense. To schedule this call, here's what to do:

Step #1—Visit **MainStreetAuthor.com**.

Step #2—Review my publishing opportunities.

Step #3—Click the Shook Strategy Session button and follow the prompts to schedule a call with me.

This one-on-one call with me will help me understand what you do and what your goals are. This call is all about helping you decide if working together to get your shook done is a good fit for both of us. It's a two-way interview to make sure we agree this is a good match.

Thank you and I look forward to speaking with you.

ABOUT MIKE CAPUZZI

M ike is a publisher, author and coach for business owners looking to get to the next level in their business. Throughout his 25 years in marketing and 21 years as a consultant, Mike's innovative use of High Impact Marketing has consistently surpassed the expectations and outcomes of traditional marketing concepts and business strategies for his clients.

This expertise has led him to be a guest speaker on the stages of some of the world's most foremost experts on marketing, including Dan Kennedy, Bill Glazer, Rory Fatt, Ed Rush and Julie Steinbacher. To date, Mike has helped thousands of business owners create more profitable marketing.

Mike is the inventor of the wildly successful software product, CopyDoodles®. CopyDoodles are hand-drawn graphic files that enable anybody to literally drag and drop attention-grabbing enhancements to their offline and online marketing materials. Tens of thousands of business owners, marketers and copywriters have benefited from the use of CopyDoodles (check out **CopyDoodles.com**).

In 2019, Mike launched Bite Sized Books, a new publishing venture founded on his proven formula for creating short, helpful books (known as shooks) for Main Street business owners. Shooks are ideal for local business owners who are looking to increase their level of authority, while also providing helpful information in bite sized books.

Mike is also the host of The Main Street Author Podcast where he interviews business owners and book experts on real-world, proven ways to leverage a book to position yourself and promote your business. Check it out at **MikeCapuzzi.com,** and if you think you would make a great guest (one that has written and published at least one printed book), visit **MikeCapuzzi.com/guest** to introduce yourself.

To learn more about Mike's opportunities, visit **MikeCapuzzi.com**, and if you're looking for a content-rich, unique speaker for your in-person or virtual event or podcast, contact Mike for his speaker kit.

THE MAIN STREET AUTHOR PODCAST

The Main Street Author Podcast is an interview-style podcast with host Mike Capuzzi and local Main Street business owners who have successfully authored, published and leveraged a book in their business to differentiate themselves and attract more ideal customers, clients, patients or students.

Each episode is focused on book strategies that work for traditional local business owners. Even though you may have never heard of some of Mike's guests, you're sure to get several ideas and nuggets of wisdom that are proven to work in the real world of face-to-face business.

Listen at **MikeCapuzzi.com** and if you think you would make a suitable guest on the Main Street Author Podcast, visit **MikeCapuzzi.com/guest** and connect with Mike.

A SMALL FAVOR

Thank you for reading *The 100-Page Book*! I am positive if you follow what I've written, you will be on your way to being a short, helpful book author! When you do, please send me a copy of your shook so I can show it off! I have a small, quick favor to ask. Would you mind taking a minute or two and leaving an honest review for this shook on Amazon? Reviews are the BEST way to help others purchase this shook, and I check all my reviews looking for helpful feedback. Visit:

100PageBook.com/review

If you have any questions or if you would just like to tell me what you think about *The 100-Page Book*, shoot an email to info@mikecapuzzi.com. I'd love to hear from you!

Made in the USA
Monee, IL
30 July 2020